Level
4

Dinosaur
Detectives

Peter Chrisp

CONTENTS

6   Dinosaur Hunters

8   The Fossil Woman

16   The Strange Tooth

22   Dinner in a Dinosaur

26   The Bone Hunters

34   The Great Bone Rush

36 The Biggest Bone Dig

40 Dating the Dinosaurs

42 Baby Dinosaurs

46 Glossary

47 Index

48 Quiz

Mary Anning
Anning was one of the first fossil hunters. See page 8.

Gideon Mantell
This English doctor found a beast he called *Iguanodon*. See page 16.

Richard Owen
This English scientist held a party inside a concrete model of a dinosaur. See page 22.

DINOSAUR HUNTERS

Long, long ago, people all over the world began finding huge bones buried in sand or stone. Sometimes, these findings gave rise to stories about giants and dragons.

Today, we know these bones belonged to enormous beasts that lived millions of years ago. Some of them were land reptiles, called dinosaurs. Dinosaurs walked Earth for over 170 million years.

The dinosaurs died out, or became extinct, 66 million years ago.

In this book, you can read about some of the people who first discovered the truth about these huge bones. Like detectives, they worked to collect evidence and put together clues.

What they learned gives us a picture of life in the far distant past, when our world was the home of the dinosaurs.

Othniel Charles Marsh
This American and his rival Edward Cope hunted for fossils in the Old West. See page 34.

Werner Janensch
This German scientist went to Africa to dig for dinosaurs. See page 36.

Jack Horner
This American scientist dug up dozens of dinosaur nests. See page 42.

Fossils Defined
Fossils are the remains of plants and animals, preserved in rock. Many fossils are bones that have gradually turned to stone.

THE FOSSIL WOMAN

Welcome to my fossil shop! My name is Mary Anning. I've lived here in Lyme Regis, England, all my life. I was born in 1799 above this very shop, where my father was a carpenter.

For six days of the week, Father worked hard, making furniture. But on Sundays, he would take me for walks along the beaches to look for fossils. He sold them to the ladies and gentlemen who come to the seaside every summer.

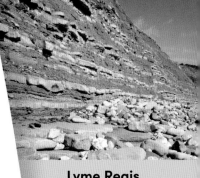

Father taught me how to tap a rock in just the right place with a hammer to make it split open.

Often, there would be nothing inside it. But sometimes we would find the skeleton of a beautiful fish or a curly shell. We call the shells "snakestones" because they look like curled-up snakes. Scientists call them ammonites.

The best time to find fossils is after a storm, when the wind and waves batter and chip away at the cliffs. When a storm hits Lyme Regis, all sorts of strange creatures just fall out of the cliffs.

Father said that we were "fishing for curiosities." It was a bit like fishing because we never knew what we would catch. But our "fish" were made of stone.

Lyme Regis
This town on the south coast of England is still one of the best places in the world to find fossils.

Fossil Seller
Mary Anning (1799–1847) was the first person to make a living by selling fossils.

Ammonites
These ancient relatives of the squid lived in the sea and caught food with their tentacles.

Seashells
Anning's fossil discoveries made her famous. The tongue twister "she sells seashells on the sea shore" is thought by some to refer to her.

Fishing
Many people in Lyme Regis made their living from fishing in the sea.

My poor father died in 1810, when I was just 10 years old. Mother made some money by selling fish, but it was not enough for us to live on.

I knew that I had to work to help feed my family. I decided that I would spend all my time looking for curiosities to sell.

One day, I was looking for fossils with my brother, Joseph Anning. Walking along the beach, I looked at the cliff and saw something wonderful staring back at me.

It was the skull of a strange animal. And what a skull!

It must have been about 4 feet (1 m) long, with a big round eyehole and jaws stuffed with sharp teeth.

"It's a sea dragon, Mary!" said Joseph excitedly.

We hammered at the rocks until we could free the skull. Although it was very heavy, we managed to carry it home.

Joseph and I looked at pictures of animals in a book to see if we could discover what it was. We decided that it must be a crocodile.

Tools
Mary used simple tools, like this hammer and chisel, to split open rocks and chip out fossils.

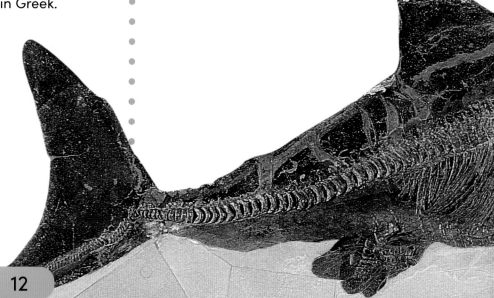

I was sure that the rest of the crocodile was still there, buried in the cliff. All I had to do was wait for another rockslide. So, after every storm, I would go back to the spot where we found the skull, hoping to see the rest of the skeleton.

It was almost a year later, in 1812, that the rocks finally fell away. There was my creature! But it wasn't a crocodile. Instead of legs, this animal had short paddles. It looked more like a fish!

I chipped the skeleton free with my hammer, and we carried it carefully back to our shop.

News quickly spread that the Annings had found a "sea dragon." Everyone wanted to have a look, and we were able to charge visitors some money to see it. Then, we sold the skeleton to a local nobleman for 23 pounds (about $29)—more money than I'd ever seen before.

At this time, I met my first geologists—scientific gentlemen who came to see the creature and argue about what it was. One of these geologists, Charles Konig, gave my creature a name: *Ichthyosaurus*.

Reptiles
This group of animals includes lizards and snakes. *Ichthyosaurus* was a reptile that swam like a fish.

Naming
Scientists give all plants and animals Greek or Latin names.

When I was 22 years old, I found an even stranger creature in the cliffs. It had a tiny head, an amazingly long neck, and four flippers.

It took me months to chip it free from the rocks, but it was time well spent. I was able to sell it to the Duke of Buckingham for 100 pounds (about $125).

I showed the skeleton to a geologist called William Conybeare, who visited me. His mouth dropped open in astonishment.

"I have never seen anything like this before!" he said. "It has the head of a turtle and the paddles of a whale. But its neck is like a giant snake. I shall call it *Plesiosaurus*, which means 'almost a reptile.'"

Plesiosaurus made me famous, although some geologists accused me of having created a fake fossil to make money.

Then, last year I discovered a reptile with wings! A fossil expert called William Buckland has named it *Pterodactylus macronyx*. He says that the poor beast must have drowned in the sea.

Of course, finds such as these are very rare. Mostly, I live by selling ammonites. Would you like to buy one?

Flying Reptiles
Anning's *Pterodactylus macronyx* was a pterosaur. Pterosaurs were flying reptiles that lived at the same time as the dinosaurs.

"Almost a Reptile"
William Conybeare published a description of the *Plesiosaurus* in 1821. He apologized for giving it such a "vague name."

Busy Doctor
Gideon Mantell (1790–1852) visited up to 60 patients a day. But he still found time to collect fossils and write a book called *The Geology of Sussex*.

Mary Ann Mantell
Mary Ann eventually lost patience with her husband's hobby. She left Gideon when his fossil collection took over their whole house!

THE STRANGE TOOTH

Ladies and gentlemen, thank you for coming to my lecture! My name is Gideon Mantell. Today, I am going to tell you about a remarkable discovery that I made in 1822.

At the time, I was a doctor in the English county of Sussex. Although I practiced medicine, my real interest was in geology. Between visits to patients, I would always find time to collect fossils.

One spring day, I was visiting a patient with my wife, Mary Ann Mantell. She had come with me to enjoy the fine weather. While I was busy, she strolled down the lane and saw a pile of rocks, used by workers to repair the roads.

In one of the rocks, Mary Ann noticed something brown and shiny. Looking closely, she saw that it was a very large tooth.

And here is that tooth! As you can see, it is worn away on the side from chewing, like the tooth of a plant-eating mammal. But it is an odd shape, with ridges. I had never seen anything like it.

The workers took me to the quarry, where I was amazed to learn that the tooth had come from a very old layer of rocks. No mammal fossil has ever been found in such rocks.

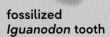

fossilized *Iguanodon* tooth

Teeth
Tooth shapes show what an animal eats. Plant eaters have short teeth for chopping and chewing leaves. Meat eaters have sharp, jagged teeth.

Rock Layers
Different types of fossils are found in different layers of rock. The oldest layers are the lowest in a rock face.

17

Buckland
William Buckland was the scientist who named Mary Anning's pterosaur.

Eccentric
Buckland kept a pet bear and often did chicken impressions in the middle of his lectures!

Clever Horse
Buckland's horse always stopped when she passed a quarry. She wouldn't move until he got off and looked for fossils.

I knew of one man who might be able to help me solve the mystery of the tooth. Only William Buckland has a bigger collection of fossils than I do. He has spent years collecting them from quarries around England.

I traveled to the professor's home in Oxford, England, and showed him the enormous tooth.

"Remarkable, sir!" said Buckland. "I fear I cannot help you to identify it. But let me show you a fossil!"

He led me to his desk, piled high with a jumble of rocks. Buckland pulled out a large bone and handed it to me.

I could see that it was a jaw, for it held a long, sharp, curved tooth. "It looks like a flesh eater," I said, "a very big flesh eater!"

"It was found in a slate quarry not far from here," said Buckland. "As you will observe, it is shaped like a lizard's jaw. Yet from the size of the tooth, this lizard must have been more than 40 feet (12 m)-long.

Think of that, sir—a 40-foot (12-m)-long flesh-eating lizard roaming around Oxfordshire!" I shuddered at the thought of it.

The professor went on, "I am going to call this great lizard a *Megalosaurus*."

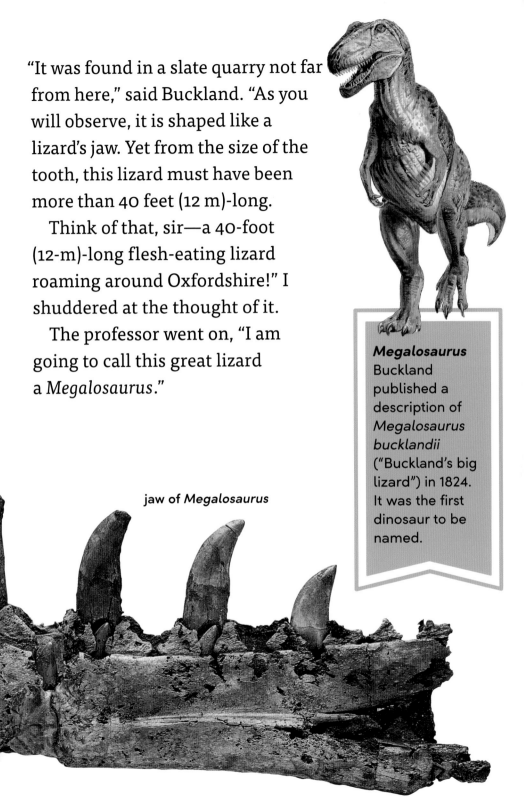

Megalosaurus
Buckland published a description of *Megalosaurus bucklandii* ("Buckland's big lizard") in 1824. It was the first dinosaur to be named.

jaw of *Megalosaurus*

Strange Meals
Buckland was famous for eating unusual animals. He always said that a mole was the most revolting thing he had ever tasted—until he ate a bluebottle fly.

Age of Reptiles
In 1838, Mantell published a book called *The Wonders of Geology*. It included this picture of a *Megalosaurus* attacking an *Iguanodon*.

Buckland invited me to stay for dinner, but I made excuses and left. I had heard that the professor ate odd things, like hedgehog meat.

As I traveled home, I thought about Buckland's discovery. I already knew of the giant sea reptiles discovered by Mary Anning at Lyme Regis. Now Buckland had found a huge land reptile.

Perhaps my tooth also came from an ancient reptile. Was it possible, I wondered, that before the time of the mammals, there had been an age of reptiles? I found my next clue in 1825 at the museum of the Royal College of Surgeons in London.

Looking through the collection of skeletons, I came across a South American lizard called an iguana. Its teeth were shaped just like the one I had found, with the same ridges. The only difference was that my tooth was 20 times bigger.

This convinced me that I had indeed found a reptile. I decided to call my reptile *Iguanodon*, or "iguana tooth."

Iguana
The South American iguana grows up to 5 feet (1.5 m) long. Mantell pictured his *Iguanodon* like an iguana, but 20 times bigger.

Iguanodon
Mantell published his description of *Iguanodon* in 1825. It was the second dinosaur to be named.

Skeleton Expert
Richard Owen was able to study many different skeletons by cutting up animals that died at the London Zoo.

Crowd Pleaser
In 1854, huge crowds went to the Crystal Palace in London to see the concrete models of *Iguanodon* and *Megalosaurus*.

Exhibition
Owen's models were the world's first dinosaur exhibition.

DINNER IN A DINOSAUR

I will never forget the party I went to in London on New Year's Eve in 1853. We ate our dinner inside an *Iguanodon*!

It was not a flesh-and-blood *Iguanodon*, of course. It was a brick and concrete model, built to show the public what these remarkable beasts might have looked like.

My name is Joseph Prestwick, and, like most of the guests on that evening, I'm a geologist.

At the head of our table sat our host, Richard Owen, an expert on animal skeletons. He had designed the splendid creature in which we sat.

Owen rose to his feet and said, "Fellow scientists! Let us drink to the memory of Gideon Mantell, discoverer of *Iguanodon*!"

We raised our glasses and cried, "Mantell!" There was a brief silence, as we each remembered the good doctor, who had died the previous year. It was sad indeed that Mantell was not there to see his discovery brought to life.

thumb

Nose Horn?
The concrete *Iguanodon* had a horn on its nose. Mantell and Owen had both misunderstood this bone. It was really the dinosaur's thumb!

As midnight approached, my friend Edward Forbes thanked our host for the splendid meal.

Forbes said, "We owe Owen a great deal, gentlemen. Gideon Mantell and William Buckland thought of their discoveries as overgrown lizards. But in the 1830s, more bones of these huge reptiles were found, and Owen studied them closely.

"Owen has a great understanding of skeletons. He could see that, unlike lizards, these creatures held their bodies off the ground on straight legs. They were not giant lizards. They were a separate group of animals, which Owen has named *Dinosauria*.

Standing Tall
Straight legs are better at bearing weight than the sprawling legs of lizards. It was thanks to their straight legs that dinosaurs could grow so much bigger than any other reptiles.

And now, if I may," Forbes added, "I would like to read you a poem that I have written. It is about this magnificent *Iguanodon* in which we are sitting.

A thousand ages underground
His skeleton had lain;
But now his body's big
and round
And he's himself again!
The jolly old beast
Is not deceased,
There's life in him again!"

At this, we all let out a huge roar like a bellowing herd of *Iguanodon*.

Dinosauria

Two Legs or Four?
Owen mistakenly believed that all dinosaurs walked on four legs. Later finds showed that many walked on their hind legs, like this *Giganotosaurus*.

Dinosaurs
In 1841, Owen invented the name "dinosaur." It means "terrible lizard" in Greek.

THE BONE HUNTERS

Expeditions
In the 1870s, Othniel Charles Marsh (1831–1899) led his students on four fossil-hunting expeditions to the West.

Railroad
In the 1860s, the Union Pacific Railroad was built across the USA to link the cities of the East with the West.

My name is Matthew Randall, but all my friends call me Matty. Let me tell you about my young days out in the American West.

Back in 1868, I found work on the building of the Union Pacific Railroad. Laying those iron rails was hard work, and it was dangerous, too. This was the homeland of the Sioux, who hated the railroad.

For months on end, we lived on fried bison steaks, provided by our own hunter, "Buffalo Bill" Cody.

One day, a group of strangers rode into our camp. There were about a dozen youngsters led by an older fellow.

"Good day," said the older man. "I am Othniel Charles Marsh of Yale University, and these are my students. We are on a bone-hunting expedition!"

This struck me as an odd occupation, although I was too polite to say so.

Buffalo Bill
William Cody earned his nickname by supplying the railway workers with bison meat. He was famous for his skill as a scout.

Sioux
The Sioux depended on bison for food, clothes, tools, and tents. The settlers and the railroad ruined Sioux hunting grounds.

Museum
Marsh was the nephew of George Peabody, a millionaire banker. He used his uncle's money to build the Peabody Museum at Yale University to house his fossils.

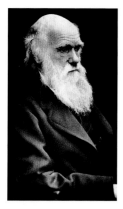

Darwin
In 1859, naturalist Charles Darwin suggested that animals are not fixed in one permanent form, or species. They change over time, to produce new species. He called this "evolution."

Marsh had come to our camp to meet up with Buffalo Bill, who had offered to be his guide on the bone-hunting expedition.

Next morning, the bone hunters rode off. Buffalo Bill led the way and Marsh rode beside him. They had an escort of cavalrymen and six wagons. We wished them well and then went back to our work on the railroad.

More than a month later, we met up with Marsh again. His students now looked like real westerners, with tanned faces and well-worn clothing.

Marsh was full of stories of his adventures. He said that he'd shot an angry bull bison that was charging at him. He'd also made friends with some Sioux, who called him "Big Bone Chief."

Then, he showed us the wagonloads of bones he'd collected. He handed one of them around.

"Here's a real treasure," he said. "It's a bird's skull with teeth in its beak! This shows that birds must have evolved from reptiles. It proves that Charles Darwin was right about evolution!"

We had no idea what he was talking about.

Bird with Teeth
Darwin's followers believed that one group of dinosaurs grew feathers and took to the air. They evolved into birds. Early birds kept some reptile features, such as teeth.

Proof
Darwin's supporters hoped to find fossils that would prove his theory. This was why Marsh was excited to find a bird's skull with teeth.

Headdress
Sioux warriors wore eagle feather headdresses.

Black Hills
The Sioux fought for the Black Hills. They won a victory at the Battle of the Little Bighorn in 1877, but eventually they lost their territory.

Marsh said that if we ever found any unusual bones, we should write to him at Yale. Then, he went home with his students and his collection of bones. I guessed that this was the last I would hear of bone hunting.

Over the next years, big changes came to the West. The railroads I helped to build brought thousands of settlers from the East. New towns sprang up all over the place.

In 1874, gold was discovered in the Black Hills in Sioux territory. Soon, we had a real gold rush, with trainloads of easterners arriving, all hoping to strike it rich. The Sioux fought to defend their land, but they were forced to move to reservations.

I'd found a job looking after the train depot at a little place called Como Bluff in Wyoming, USA. I had plenty of free time and I'd often walk up into the hills.

There wasn't much to look at there—just a lot of dry, bare rocks.

But one day in 1877, I found a bone sticking out of the rocks that was bigger than I was! Nearby, there was another huge bone, and another. These bones seemed to go on for miles.

Teepees
Before they were forced to stay on reservations, the Sioux made good use of portable homes called teepees. These were made of bison hide stretched over wooden poles.

Bare Rocks
The rocky hills of Wyoming, USA, have been worn away by rivers, rain, and wind. These areas, called badlands, are wonderful places to find fossils.

Cope
Edward Drinker Cope (1840–1897) wrote more than 1,400 books and articles and named more than 1,000 new animal species.

Spies
Both Marsh and Cope hired spies to keep an eye on what the other one was doing. They also used bribes to win over diggers from the rival team.

I was going to send a letter to Marsh, but then I heard that a rich bone-hunting professor had arrived in Canon City, not far away.

I traveled there, expecting to find Marsh. But I was surprised to see a different fellow. He said his name was Edward Drinker Cope.

I asked him if he knew Marsh. "Marsh!" shouted Cope, turning red in the face. "The man is a fraud and a thief!" It seemed that Cope hated Marsh worse than poison.

When I told him about the bones I had found, he offered me $100. I had to show him the place and keep it a secret from Marsh's spies.

Cope soon had a team of diggers at work, blasting the rock with gunpowder and prying the bones out with crowbars. Many bones shattered and were thrown away.

But Cope couldn't keep his secret forever. One day, a team of Marsh's diggers showed up. It was just like the days of the gold rush, only these fellows were after bones.

Broken Bones
Eventually, the diggers invented ways to protect the bones they dug up. Marsh's men wrapped them in strips of cloth, soaked in flour and water. Cope's men used boiled rice instead of flour.

Useful Technique
The practice of wrapping fossils in cloth and plaster of Paris is still used on some digs today.

THE GREAT BONE RUSH

Cope and Marsh each had teams of diggers working all over the West. It was a race to describe and name all the new species. As a result of this "bone rush," they discovered almost 130 new kinds of dinosaur.

Cope worked alone, but Marsh had a team of expert assistants to help him put the skeletons together.

Marsh's dinosaurs came in many shapes and sizes. There was the flesh-eating *Allosaurus* ("different reptile") and gigantic plant eaters like the *Barosaurus* ("heavy reptile").

Triceratops

There were also dinosaurs with horns, such as the *Triceratops* ("three-horned face").

The strangest dinosaur of all was one Marsh called *Stegosaurus* ("roofed reptile"). It had rows of mysterious bony plates all along its back.

Meanwhile, Cope and Marsh attacked each other in newspaper articles. Their squabbling made both of them look silly, but it also made "dinosaur" a household word.

Roofed Reptile
Scientists still argue about what the *Stegosaurus* used its plates for. Some think they helped the animal control its temperature. Others believe they were used to signal to other dinosaurs.

Allosaurus

Stegosaurus

Life's Work
Werner Janensch
(1878–1969)
spent the rest of
his life working
on the bones he
brought back
from Africa.

Leg Bone
Brachiosaurus
was so big that its
femur (upper leg
bone) was as
long as a person!

THE BIGGEST BONE DIG

My name is Werner Janensch. I've just come home to Germany after spending three years in Africa, leading a huge dig.

Back in 1907, I heard that some giant bones had been found at a place called Tendaguru in East Africa. I raised the money for an expedition and sailed to Africa in 1909.

I hired hundreds of local people to help me with the project. Tendaguru lies far inland, and there are no roads. All our food and supplies had to be carried on foot from the coast. The bones we dug up had to be carried back in the same way.

I was expecting to find new dinosaurs in Africa.

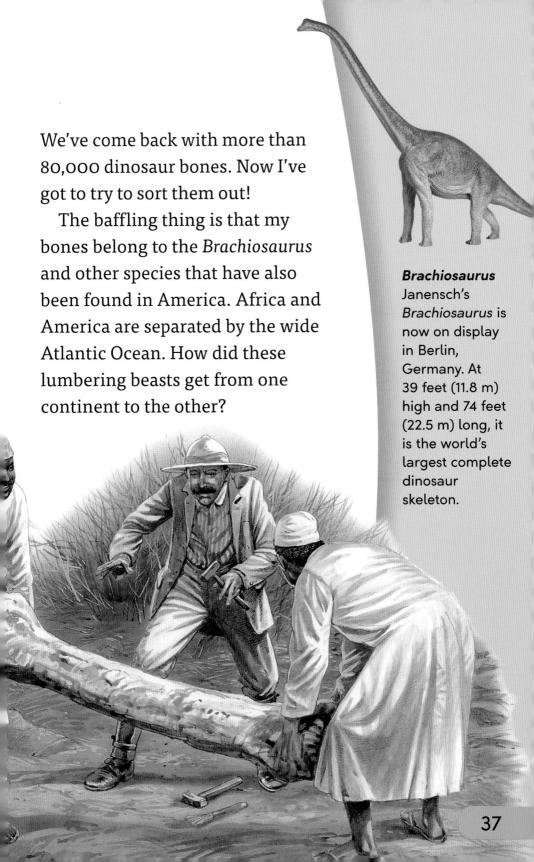

We've come back with more than 80,000 dinosaur bones. Now I've got to try to sort them out!

The baffling thing is that my bones belong to the *Brachiosaurus* and other species that have also been found in America. Africa and America are separated by the wide Atlantic Ocean. How did these lumbering beasts get from one continent to the other?

Brachiosaurus
Janensch's *Brachiosaurus* is now on display in Berlin, Germany. At 39 feet (11.8 m) high and 74 feet (22.5 m) long, it is the world's largest complete dinosaur skeleton.

In Berlin, Germany, I showed my *Brachiosaurus* skull to some of our geologists. "This is an American dinosaur," I explained. "How did it end up in Africa? It's a mystery!"

Most of them were puzzled. But a young man called Alfred Wegener said, "It's not a mystery at all. This is exactly the type of dinosaur I would expect to find in Africa!"

Wegener pulled out a world map. "Look at the coastlines of Africa and South America. Their shapes match exactly. I believe that they must have once been joined.

Wegener
In 1912, Alfred Wegener suggested that there was once only one huge landmass, which he called "Pangaea." He believed that it had split into pieces. The pieces slowly drifted apart to form the continents that we know today.

Wild Theory
At the time, few scientists took Wegener's theory of "continental drift" seriously. It was not until the 1960s that he was proved right.

Somehow, they have drifted to their present positions.

"This is why you found the same dinosaurs in Africa and America. When your *Brachiosaurus* was alive, there was no Atlantic Ocean!"

We were all startled by this wild theory. "Are you seriously suggesting that continents can roam around Earth's surface?" I asked. "How is this possible?"

"I don't know," said Wegener. "But your *Brachiosaurus* is the proof that I am right!"

Drifting Continents
We now know that Earth's surface is made up of several enormous plates floating on top of molten rock. Forces inside Earth move the plates slowly. This is what made the continents move and split apart.

Pangaea

270 million years ago

South America — Africa

130 million years ago

Present day

DATING THE DINOSAURS

Triassic
(252–201 million years ago)
Early dinosaurs, like this small *Herrerasaurus*, evolved in the Triassic period.

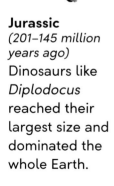

Jurassic
(201–145 million years ago)
Dinosaurs like *Diplodocus* reached their largest size and dominated the whole Earth.

Like detectives, early geologists collected evidence to piece together the story of life on Earth. Using fossils, they were able to place different periods of Earth's history in order. They gave these periods names based on the type of rocks in which the various fossils were found.

The age of the dinosaurs was divided into three periods: Triassic, when dinosaurs first evolved; Jurassic, when they became the main land animals; and Cretaceous, when new sorts, such as the horned dinosaurs, appeared.

Geologists knew that Triassic dinosaurs must have lived before Jurassic ones. But they could only guess how long ago that was.

It was not until the 1920s that scientists were able to work out the age of rocks. This was thanks to the study of radioactivity.

Many rocks are made up of elements that are radioactive. These elements slowly decay, or break down, to form other elements. Scientists measure the amount of a radioactive element in a rock. They can then work out how long the decay has been going on and so when the rock was formed.

Radioactive decay is like a clock, ticking away inside Earth's rocks. Using this clock, scientists were able to date the rocks that held the dinosaur fossils.

This told them when the dinosaurs had lived.

Cretaceous
(145–66 million years ago)
This was the age of the horned dinosaurs, such as this *Protoceratops*.

Elements
Elements are the basic substances, such as carbon, potassium, and uranium, that all things are made of.

Jack Horner
Jack Horner (1946–) is one of the world's leading experts on dinosaurs. He was the technical adviser for the films *Jurassic Park* and *The Lost World*.

Paleontology
A modern dinosaur detective is called a paleontologist. Paleontology is the study of ancient life. It comes from the Greek word *palaios*, which means "ancient."

BABY DINOSAURS

In 1978, a paleontologist named Jack Horner was visiting a fossil shop in Montana, USA. He found the bones of a baby dinosaur. This was an important discovery. Few baby dinosaurs had ever been found!

Horner traced the fossil back to the rocky hillside where it had been discovered and began to dig. Soon, he had uncovered a huge nest. It was over 6 feet (2 m) wide and contained 15 baby dinosaurs and lots of crushed eggshells.

In the 1980s, Horner's team found more nests at the site. Some of them contained eggs and newly hatched babies.

Horner knew that the soil around the nests could hold clues.

By sifting the soil and examining it under a microscope, he discovered the remains of chewed-up leaves and berries. He also found dinosaur droppings, containing woody debris from conifer trees. Can you work out what he discovered?

Horner used these clues and other evidence to build an amazing picture of the lives of these dinosaurs.

Fossilized Baby Horner's team chipped away the rock to discover this fossilized eggshell containing a baby hatchling.

Herds
Fossil footprints are further evidence that some dinosaurs, such as these *Gallimimus*, traveled in herds. The young stayed in the middle of a herd, while the adults walked on either side to provide protection.

Horner's most important discovery was that the babies were being looked after by their parents. He called this dinosaur *Maiasaura*, which means "good mother lizard."

The evidence for parental care was the size of the 15 babies. Since they were three times bigger than newly hatched ones, they must have stayed in their nest for weeks after hatching. They had crushed the eggshells in their nest as they moved around. The chewed-up leaves and berries were food brought by the parents.

The mystery is why the babies died. Perhaps something happened to their parents, and the babies starved to death in the nest.

In 1984, Horner's team made another discovery. They found the bones of 10,000 *Maiasaura* that had been killed by a volcanic eruption. Finding so many animals together shows that they lived in huge herds.

GLOSSARY

Ammonite
A prehistoric sea creature with a coiled shell

Continental drift
The theory that the continents were once joined together, split apart, and drifted to their present positions

Cretaceous
The third period in the age of dinosaurs, 145 to 66 million years ago

Dinosaurs
Land reptiles that lived on Earth for over 170 million years and died out 66 million years ago

Elements
The basic substances, such as hydrogen, carbon, and iron, that all things are made of

Evolution
The theory that species of animals and plants gradually change over long periods of time to produce new species

Extinct
No longer existing

Fossils
Traces of animals and plants, preserved in rocks, including bones, skin, and footprints

Geology
The study of Earth and its rocks

Jurassic
The second period in the age of dinosaurs, 201 to 145 million years ago

Mammals
A group of warm-blooded animals with hair. Mammals give birth to live young, which feed on milk.

Naturalist
A scientist who studies animals and plants

Paleontology
The study of ancient life, from the Greek word *palaios*, which means "ancient"

Pterosaurs
Flying reptiles that lived at the same time as the dinosaurs

Quarry
A place where stone is dug out of the ground

Radioactivity
The energy released by elements, such as uranium, as they break down, or decay. Radioactivity can be used to date rocks.

Reptiles
A group of cold-blooded, egg-laying animals with scaly skins

Sauropods
A group of huge, long-necked dinosaurs

Species
A group of animals or plants that can breed together and that share few differences

Triassic
The first period in the age of dinosaurs, 252 to 201 million years ago

INDEX

age of reptiles 20
Allosaurus 34
ammonites 9
Anning, Joseph 10, 11
Anning, Mary 6, 8–15, 20
baby dinosaurs 42–45
Barosaurus 34
birds, with teeth 29
bones 31–33
Brachiosaurus 36–39
Buckland, William 15,
 18–20, 24
Cody, William "Buffalo
 Bill" 27, 28
continental drift 38–39
Conybeare, William
 14–15
Cope, Edward Drinker 7,
 32–35
Cretaceous period 40, 41
Darwin, Charles 28, 29
dating dinosaurs 40–41
dinosaur, invention of
 name 25
dinosaur models 22
Diplodocus 40
Earth
 history 40, 41
 plates 39
eggs 42–45
elements 41
evolution 28, 29
films 42
fishing 10
flying reptiles 14, 15
footprints 44
Forbes, Professor 24–25

fossils 8–9, 17, 33
Gallimimus 44
geology 12
Giganotosaurus 25
herds 44, 45
Herrerasaurus 40
Horner, Jack 7, 42–45
horns 23, 35
Ichthyosaurus 12, 13
iguana 21
Iguanodon 17, 20, 21,
 22–25
Janensch, Werner 7,
 36–39
jaws 18–19
Jurassic period 40
legs 24, 25, 36
lizards 13, 19, 21
Lyme Regis, England 8,
 9, 10, 20
Maiasaura 44, 45
Mantell, Gideon 6, 16–21,
 23, 24
Mantell, Mary Ann 16
Marsh, Othniel Charles 7,
 26–35
meat-eaters 17, 18
Megalosaurus 19, 20, 22
naming plants and
 animals 13
nests 42–45
Owen, Richard 6, 22–25
paleontology 42
Pangaea 38
parental care 44
Peabody Museum, Yale
 University 28

plant-eaters 17
plates 35
Plesiosaurus 15
Protoceratops 41
Pterodactyl macronyx
 14, 15
pterosaurs 14, 15
quarry 17, 18, 19
radioactivity 41
railroads 26, 27, 30
Randall, Matthew 26–33
reptiles
 age of 20
 defined 13
 flying reptiles 14, 15
reservations 30, 31
rocks
 dating 41
 layers 17
 splitting 9
sauropods 34
Sioux 26, 27, 28, 30, 31
skeletons 12, 22, 24, 37
skulls 10–11
Stegosaurus 35
teeth 16–18, 20–21, 29
thumb 23
tools for fossil hunting 11
Triassic period 40
Triceratops 35
Wegener, Alfred 38–39

QUIZ

Answer the questions to see what you have learned. Check your answers in the key below.

1. When was the best time for Mary Anning to find fossils?

2. In 1812, Anning dug up a "sea dragon." What kind of fossil was it?

3. What did Gideon Mantell call his land reptile?

4. What did the bone that Othniel Charles Marsh showed Matthew Randall look like?

5. Who invented the name "dinosaur"?

6. Alfred Wegener thought that Werner Janensch's discovery was proof of what?

7. What is the study of ancient life called?

8. What was Jack Horner's most important discovery?

1. After a storm 2. An *Ichthyosaurus* 3. An *Iguanodon* or "iguana tooth"
4. A bird's skull with teeth 5. Richard Owen 6. Continental drift
7. Paleontology 8. Dinosaur babies were looked after by their parents